TABLE OF CONTENTS

T0015114

CHAPTER 1

HEY, DRAGONFLY!

Four wings **flutter**. Two big, round eyes see all the way around. They see more colors than people do! What is this **insect**? It is a dragonfly!

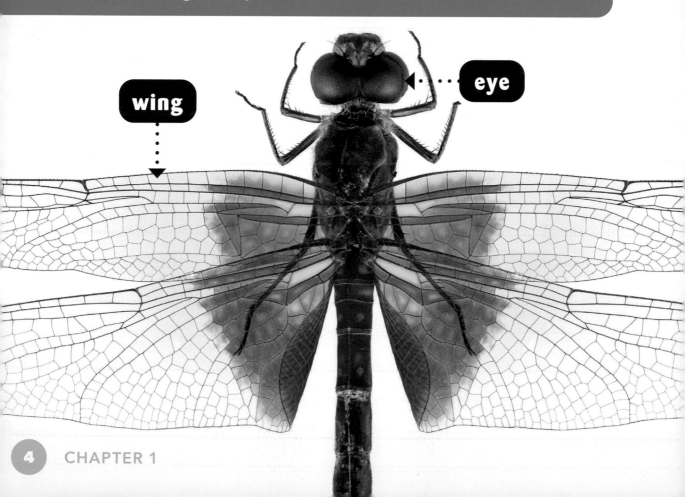

wing

eye

ALL ABOUT INSECTS
ALL ABOUT DRAGONFLIES

by Karen Latchana Kenney

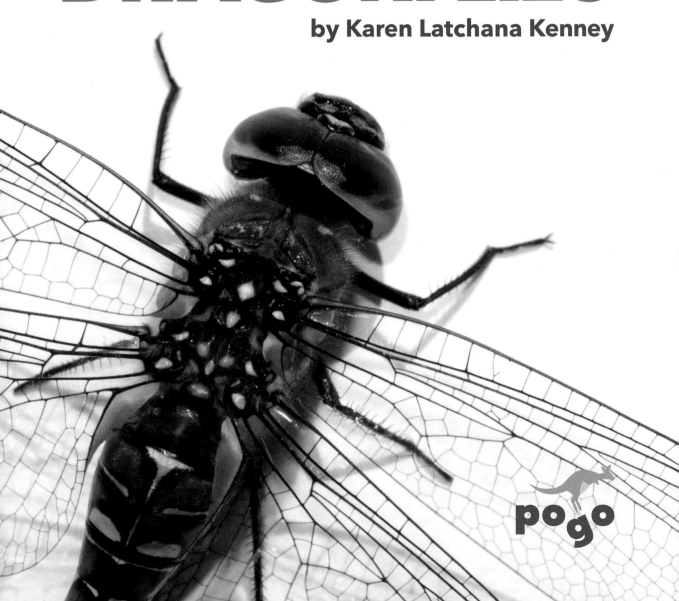

pogo

Ideas for Parents and Teachers

Pogo Books let children practice reading informational text while introducing them to nonfiction features such as headings, labels, sidebars, maps, and diagrams, as well as a table of contents, glossary, and index.

Carefully leveled text with a strong photo match offers early fluent readers the support they need to succeed.

Before Reading

- "Walk" through the book and point out the various nonfiction features. Ask the student what purpose each feature serves.
- Look at the glossary together. Read and discuss the words.

Read the Book

- Have the child read the book independently.
- Invite him or her to list questions that arise from reading.

After Reading

- Discuss the child's questions. Talk about how he or she might find answers to those questions.
- Prompt the child to think more. Ask: As nymphs, dragonflies live in water. Did you know this before reading this book? What more would you like to learn about dragonflies?

Pogo Books are published by Jump!
5357 Penn Avenue South
Minneapolis, MN 55419
www.jumplibrary.com

Library of Congress Cataloging-in-Publication Data

Names: Kenney, Karen Latchana, author.
Title: All about dragonflies / by Karen Latchana Kenney.
Description: Minneapolis, MN: Jump!, Inc., [2024]
Series: All about insects | Includes index.
Audience: Ages 7-10
Identifiers: LCCN 2022051911 (print)
LCCN 2022051912 (ebook)
ISBN 9798885244305 (hardcover)
ISBN 9798885244312 (paperback)
ISBN 9798885244329 (ebook)
Subjects: LCSH: Dragonflies—Juvenile literature.
Classification: LCC QL520 .K46 2024 (print)
LCC QL520 (ebook)
DDC 595.7/33—dc23/eng/20221031
LC record available at https://lccn.loc.gov/2022051911
LC ebook record available at https://lccn.loc.gov/2022051912

Editor: Jenna Gleisner
Designer: Emma Almgren-Bersie

Photo Credits: vnlit/iStock, cover; BettinaRitter/iStock, 1; Lopatin Anton/Shutterstock, 3; Domiciano Pablo Romero Franco/Dreamstime, 4; yod 67/Shutterstock, 5; NaturesThumbPrint/iStock, 6-7; Haiduchyk Aliaksei/Shutterstock, 8-9; Frank Lane Picture Agency/SuperStock, 10; Avalon.red/Alamy, 11; Matt Cole/Shutterstock, 12-13; Wirestock/iStock, 14-15; anat chant/Shutterstock, 16 (dragonfly); Kati Finell/Shutterstock, 16 (flowers); Andyworks/iStock, 17; I Wayan Sumatika/Shutterstock, 18-19; imageBROKER/Alamy, 20-21; Antagain/iStock, 23.

Printed in the United States of America at Corporate Graphics in North Mankato, Minnesota.

There are more than 7,000 kinds of dragonflies! They can be bright and colorful. The crimson marsh glider is dark pink. It lives in Southeast Asia.

crimson marsh glider

Dragonflies have thin bodies. They can be up to five inches (13 centimeters) long. They have two sets of wings that help them fly through the air.

TAKE A LOOK!

What are the parts of a dragonfly? Take a look!

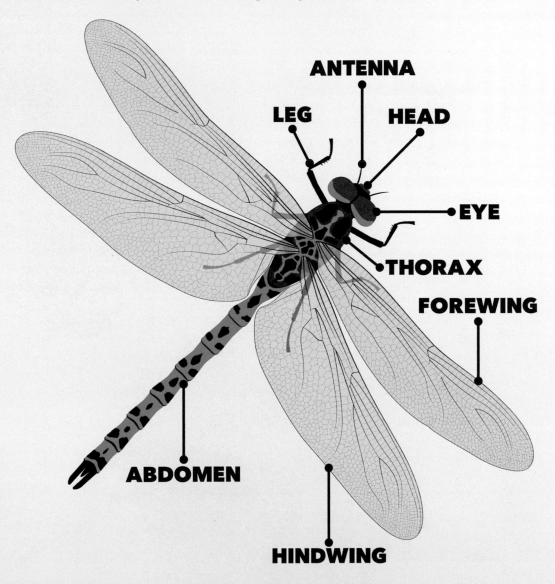

ANTENNA

LEG

HEAD

EYE

THORAX

FOREWING

ABDOMEN

HINDWING

Dragonflies live by bodies of fresh water. These include lakes, ponds, and rivers. Many live in warm **habitats**.

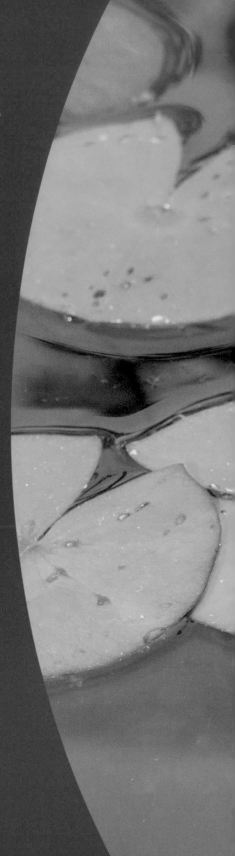

DID YOU KNOW?

Dragonflies were on Earth before dinosaurs! They were much bigger then. **Fossils** show wings almost three feet (0.9 meters) long from tip to tip.

CHAPTER 2

WATER AND AIR

Dragonflies start out living in water. Some dragonflies lay their eggs in fresh water. Others lay eggs near the water.

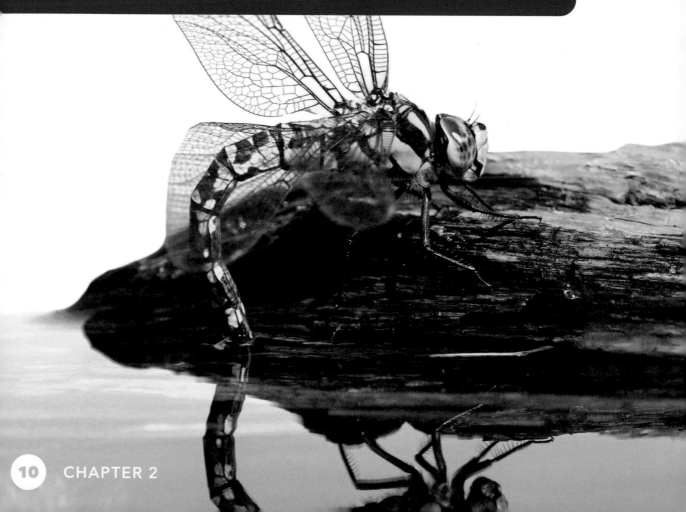

Nymphs hatch from the eggs. They live and hunt in the water. A nymph has a special lower jaw. The jaw reaches out and grabs food. Nymphs eat insects and mosquito **larvae**. They also eat small fish and **tadpoles**.

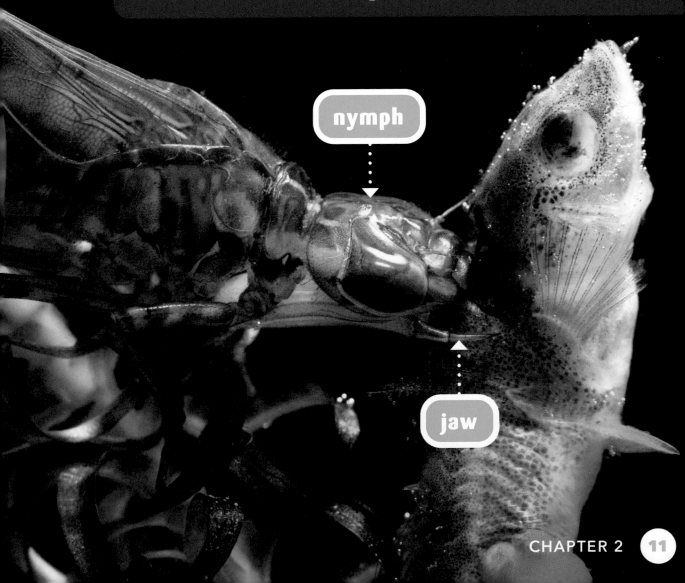

nymph

jaw

After a few years, a nymph comes out of the water. It **molts**. Now it is an adult dragonfly! It has wings.

molting
nymph

The dragonfly sits in the Sun.
It **perches** on a plant or a rock.
It stretches its wings. The Sun
dries its wings so it can fly.

CHAPTER 3

FLYING HUNTERS

A dragonfly **hovers**. It flies up, down, and side to side. It flies backward and forward, too.

This master flier hunts for **prey**. Its large eyes see everything that moves. It picks out one insect from a **swarm**. It flies after its prey.

The dragonfly grabs the insect with its feet and eats it.

Dragonflies are one of nature's best **predators**. They catch almost all prey they hunt. They eat gnats, bees, and other insects.

DID YOU KNOW?

Dragonflies fly and see well. But they cannot always escape predators. Birds, bats, and lizards catch and eat them.

Dragonflies sometimes gather in a swarm. Thousands might be in one group. They hunt together.

Have you seen a dragonfly on the hunt?

DID YOU KNOW?

Dragonflies are good fliers. **Engineers** design robots and drones to fly like them.

ACTIVITIES & TOOLS

DRAGONFLY FLIER

Dragonflies twist their wings as they fly. This is a bit like a helicopter. Make a flier that moves like a dragonfly in this fun activity!

What You Need:

- empty cereal box
- ruler
- pencil
- scissors
- hole punch
- plastic straw
- tape

1. Measure and draw a rectangle on the cereal box. The rectangle should be 1.5 inches (3.8 cm) wide and 8 inches (20 cm) long.

2. Cut out the rectangle. Then cut each short end into a rounded shape. This will be the wing.

3. Punch a hole in the center of the wing.

4. Push the straw through the hole so it sticks out 1 inch (2.5 cm) above the wing.

5. Tape the top part of the straw to the wing.

6. To make it fly, hold the bottom part of the straw between your palms. Rub your hands together to make it spin. While still rubbing, aim the flier away from you. Then, let it go. Does it fly?

GLOSSARY

engineers: People who are specially trained to design and build machines or large structures.

flutter: To move back and forth very quickly.

fossils: Traces of animals or plants from millions of years ago preserved as rock.

habitats: The places where animals or plants are usually found.

hovers: Remains in one place in the air.

insect: A small animal with three pairs of legs, one or two pairs of wings, and three main body parts.

larvae: Insects in the stage of growth between eggs and pupae.

molts: Sheds an old, outer skin so that a new one can grow.

nymphs: Young dragonflies in the larvae stage.

perches: Sits or stands on something.

predators: Animals that hunt other animals for food.

prey: Animals that are hunted by other animals for food.

swarm: A large group of flying insects.

tadpoles: Young frogs that live in water and have long tails but no legs.

INDEX

TO LEARN MORE

Finding more information is as easy as 1, 2, 3.

① Go to www.factsurfer.com

② Enter "dragonflies" into the search box.

③ Choose your book to see a list of websites.

FACT SURFER